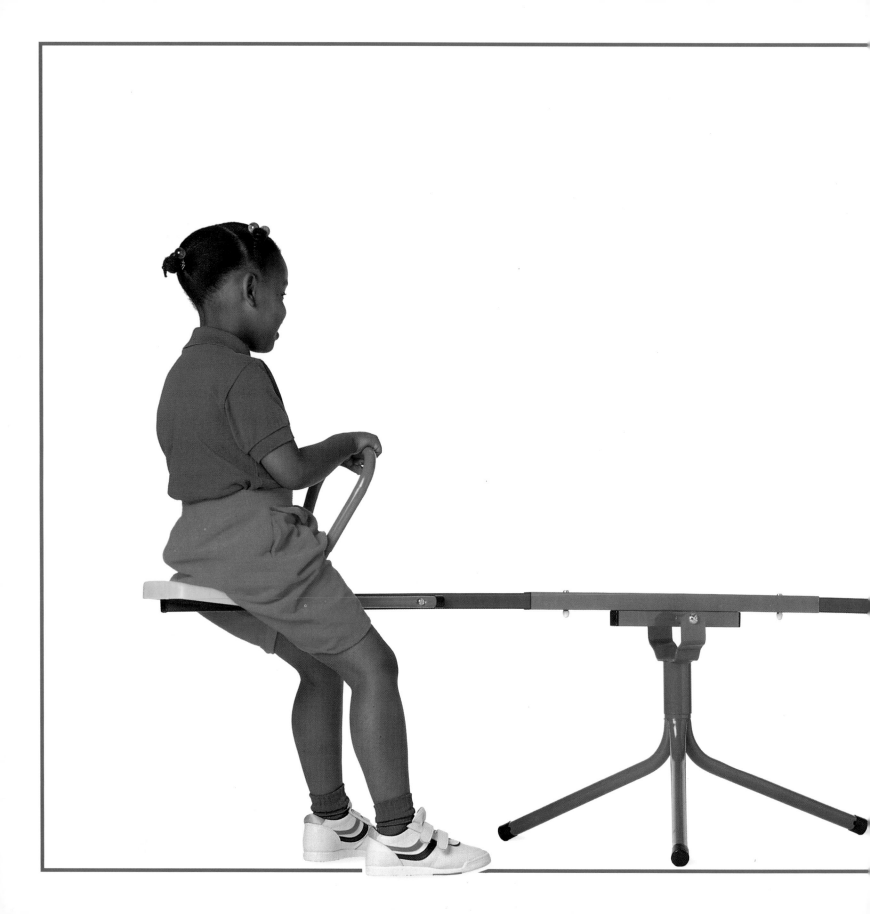

◆ LET'S EXPLORE SCIENCE ◑

Make it Balance

▲ David Evans and Claudette Williams ☐

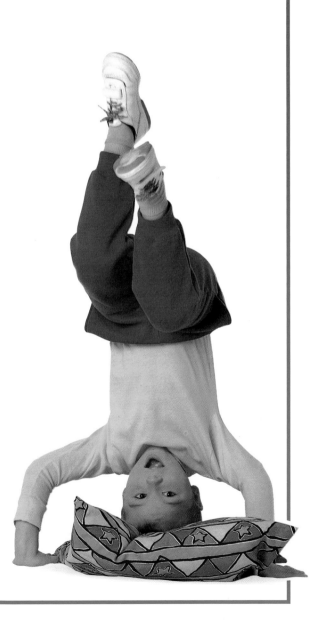

Scholastic Canada Ltd

A DORLING KINDERSLEY BOOK

Project Editor Dawn Sirett
Art Editor Karen Fielding
Managing Editor Jane Yorke
Managing Art Editor Chris Scollen
Production Jayne Wood
Photography by Susanna Price

First published in Great Britain in 1992
by Dorling Kindersley Limited,
9 Henrietta Street, London WC2E 8PS

Published in Canada in 1992
by Scholastic Canada Ltd.,
123 Newkirk Road, Richmond Hill, Ontario,
Canada L4C 3G5

Canadian Cataloguing in Publication Data
Evans, David, 1937-
Make it balance
(Let's explore science)
Includes index.
ISBN 0-590-74510-7
1. Balance – Juvenile literature. 2. Balance –
Experiments – Juvenile literature. I. Williams,
Claudette. II. Title. III. Series: Let's explore
science (Richmond Hill, Ont.).
QC107.E83 1992   j530.8   C92-094430-2

Reproduced by J. Film Process Singapore Pte., Ltd.
Printed and bound in Belgium by Proost

Dorling Kindersley would like to thank the following for their help in
producing this book: Steve Shott (for additional photography); Coral Mula
(for safety symbol artwork); Mark Richards; Yael Freudmann; Roger Priddy;
Chris Legee; Rowena Alsey; Jane Coney; Julia Fletcher; Jenny Vaughan;
the Futcher School, Drayton, Portsmouth; St. Clements Danes Church of
England Primary School, London; and Rosemary Sirett. Dorling Kindersley
would also like to give special thanks to the following for appearing in this
book: Natalie Agada; Hannah Capleton; Karen Edwards; Sapphire Elia;
Leigh Hamilton; Tonya Kamil; William Lindsay; Tony Locke; Gemma
Loke; Rachael Malicki; Richard Monan; Chloe O'Connor; Tebedge
Ricketts; Jay Sprake; and John Walden.

Contents

Note to parents
and teachers 8

Can you balance? 10

Can you balance
on things? 12

Will it balance? 14

Will it topple over? 16

Does it balance? 18

Will the tray balance? 20

Can you make a mobile? 22

Will the buckets balance? 24

How well can you balance? 26

Index and Guide to experiments 28

Note to parents and teachers

Young children are forever asking questions about the things they see, touch, hear, smell, and taste. The **Let's Explore Science** series aims to foster children's natural curiosity, and encourages them to use their senses to find out about science. Each book features a variety of experiments based on one topic, which draw on a young child's everyday experiences. By investigating familiar activities, such as bouncing a ball, making cakes, or clapping hands, young children will learn that science plays an important part in the world around them.

Investigative approach
Young children can only begin to understand science if they are stimulated to think and to find out for themselves. For these reasons, an open-ended questioning approach is used in the **Let's Explore Science** books and, wherever possible, results of experiments are not shown. Children are encouraged to make their own scientific discoveries, and to interpret them according to their own ideas. This investigative approach to learning makes science exciting and not just about acquiring "facts." It will assist children in many areas of their education.

Using the books
Before starting an experiment, check the text and pictures to ensure that you have gathered any necessary equipment. Allow children to help in this process and to suggest materials to use. Once ready, it is important to let children decide how to carry out the experiment and what the result means to them. You can help by asking questions, such as "What do you think will happen?" or "What did you do?"

Household equipment

All the experiments can be carried out easily at home. In most cases, inexpensive household objects and materials are used.

Guide to experiments

The *Guide to experiments* on pages 28-29 is intended to help parents, teachers, or helpers using this book with children. It gives an outline of the scientific principles underlying the experiments, includes useful tips for carrying out the activities, suggests alternative equipment to use, and additional activities to try.

Safe experimenting

This symbol appears next to experiments where children may require adult supervision or assistance, such as when they are heating things or using sharp tools.

About this book

In **Make it Balance**, young children investigate their own physical ability to balance and are challenged to find ways to balance a variety of objects. Ideas about mass are introduced by asking children to compare heavy and light objects.

The experiments enable children to discover that:

- an object has a balancing point (this can be directly above or below its center of gravity, also known as the center of mass – where most of an object's mass appears to be concentrated);

- an object is subject to the force of gravity and, in certain circumstances, this force will cause it to topple over;

- to balance an object, opposing forces must be balanced by changing the object's position or lowering its center of gravity;

- objects with a low center of gravity, i.e., objects that are heavier at the base, tend to be more stable.

With your help, young children will enjoy exploring the world of science and discover that finding out is fun.

David Evans and Claudette Williams

Can you balance?

Try these experiments to see how well you and your friends can balance.

On a hand and foot
Can you balance like this? How high can you lift your leg and arm?

On one leg
Can you stand on one leg? Can you balance while you count to ten?

Along a line

Can you walk along a line and keep your balance? Is it easy to do if you shut your eyes?

On tiptoe

Can you balance on tiptoe?

With your eyes closed

Sit on the floor with your arms and legs crossed and your eyes closed. Can you stand up?

On your head

Can you stand on your head and straighten your legs?

Can you balance on things?

Can you balance on different things without falling off?

On uneven blocks
Can you stand on two things of uneven height?

Can you keep your balance?

On a low wall
Can you balance on a low wall and walk along? Try carrying a broom, or plastic bottles filled with water.

Over a bar
Can you balance
like this over a
low bar?

On a scooter
How long
can you
balance on
a scooter?

On stilts
Can you keep
your balance on
bucket-stilts?

13

Will it balance?

Try balancing different things on parts of your body. Which ones are easy? Which ones are hard?

On your head
Can you balance a pillow on your head?

On one finger
Can you balance a toothbrush, a plastic plate, or a ruler on one finger?

On your feet
What can you balance on the soles of your feet? Is it harder if you use one foot?

14

As you stand up

Can you stand up with a book balanced on your head? Is it easier with your arms folded?

On your knee

Can you balance a ball or a book on your knee and count to five?

On your hand

Can you balance a broom on your hand? Now try balancing it on the top of your foot. Which is easier to do?

15

Will it topple over?

Can you balance things on top of each other and build a tower?

Cup tower
How many plastic cups can you balance on one hand?

Tall tower
Can you build a tower that is taller than you are?

Book tower

Try building a tower with books and plastic cups. Can you make it balance?

Toppling books

How many books can you stack on the edge of a table before they fall?

Toppling toy

Can you make a toy that never falls over? Use a plastic lid that has a curved top.

Put a lump of modeling clay inside the lid. To make a bird, cut out and stick on a cardboard head and tail. Can you knock the bird over?

Does it balance?

Try making these different toys. Can you make them balance?

Tightrope walker
Can you make a tightrope walker? Cut a figure out of cardboard. Does it balance on a piece of string?

Now stick lumps of modeling clay onto the figure. Where do you have to put the clay to make the figure balance?

Rocking snake

Cut a snake out of cardboard. Can you make the snake balance and rock on your finger?

If you stick a lump of modeling clay onto the snake, does it help the snake balance? Where is the best place to stick the clay?

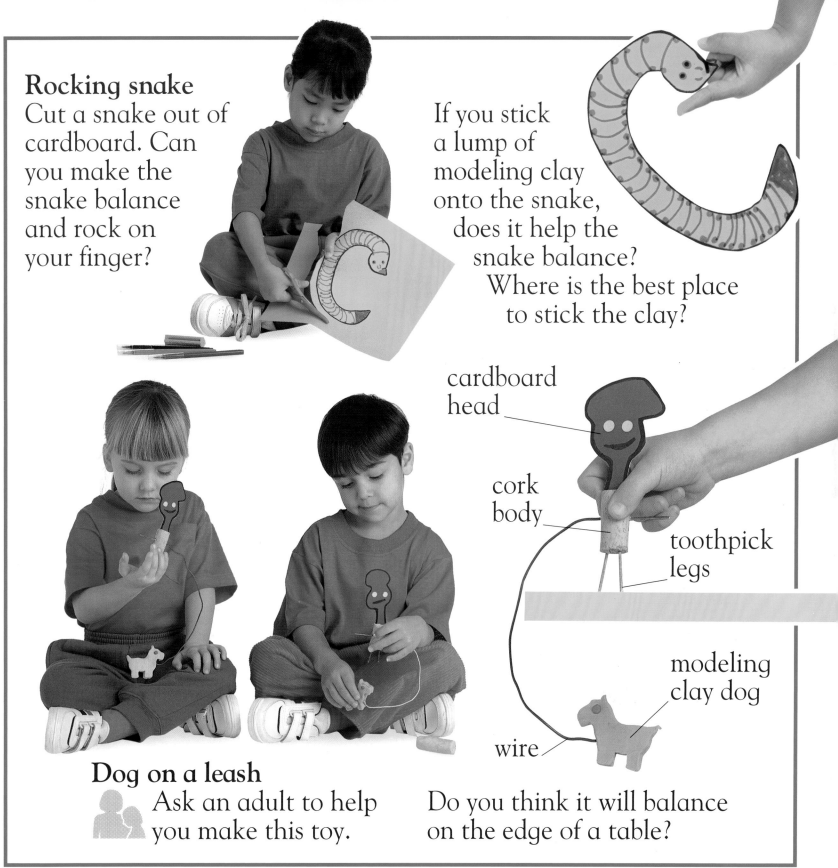

cardboard head

cork body

toothpick legs

modeling clay dog

wire

Dog on a leash
Ask an adult to help you make this toy.

Do you think it will balance on the edge of a table?

Will the tray balance?

Can you balance a tray on one hand?
Where do you have to put your hand
to make the tray balance?

Balancing cups
Put one plastic cup
on the end of a
tray. Can you make
the tray balance?

Now try two
cups. Does the
tray balance?

What happens
if you put a third
cup on the tray?

20

Balancing the tray

Can you balance a long tray on a rolling pin? Can you find some objects to put on the tray that will make it balance?

Moving the rolling pin

Will the tray balance if you put different objects on each end? What happens if you move the rolling pin?

Moving the objects

Does moving the objects help balance the tray?

Can you make a mobile?

Make your own mobile, using a coat hanger, string, tape, toys, and cardboard cutouts.

Making a mobile
Drape pieces of string over a hanger. Tape a small toy onto each piece of string.

What happens if you move the toys to different places on the hanger? Can you make the hanger balance?

Balancing a mobile

Can you make a really big mobile that balances?

Use string and tape to attach pencils or sticks to a hanger. Hang small toys and cardboard cutouts from the sticks or pencils.

Can you make heavy toys balance light toys?

Will the buckets balance?

Find out if things are heavy or light by using a bucket-balance.

Finding things to balance
Find some different objects to balance. Can you tell which things are heavier than others before you put them in a bucket-balance?

toy lion

toy car

pasta

rice

oranges

bananas

Balancing buckets

To make a bucket-balance, hook two small buckets onto a sturdy hanger. Put some of your objects into the buckets. What happens when you lift up the bucket-balance?

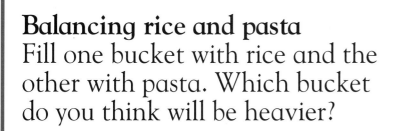

Balancing rice and pasta

Fill one bucket with rice and the other with pasta. Which bucket do you think will be heavier?

Balancing bananas and water

How much water do you need to balance a bunch of bananas?

How well can you balance?

Try these experiments to see if you are good at balancing!

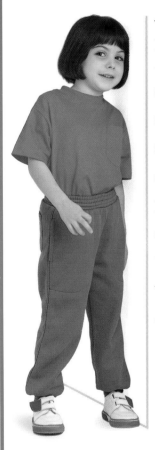

Leg lifting
Lean against a wall. Make sure your foot, arm, leg, and one side of your face and body are touching the wall. Can you lift your other leg?

Skateboarding
How far can you go on a skateboard? Is it harder to keep your balance when the skateboard stops moving?

Balancing a seesaw

What do you think will happen if you sit on one end of a seesaw and two of your friends sit on the other end?

Building a tower

Can you build a tower with playing cards? Can you balance the last cards without the tower falling down?

Toppling dominoes

How many dominoes can you stand in a row before they topple over?

Index

arms folded 11, 15
balancing points 18, 19, 20, 21, 22, 23
ball 14, 15
bananas 24, 25
bar 13
books 15, 17
broom 12, 15
bucket-balance 24, 25
coat hanger 22, 23, 25
dominoes 27
eyes closed 11
finger balances 14, 19
foot balances 10, 11, 14, 15
hand balances 10, 15, 16, 20
head balances 11, 14, 15
heavy 23, 24, 25
knee balances 15
leg balances 10, 26
light 23, 24
low wall 12
mobile 22, 23
oranges 24
pasta 24, 25
pillow 14
plastic bottles 12
plastic cups 16, 17, 20

plastic plate 14
playing cards 27
rice 24, 25
ruler 14
scooter 13
seesaw 27
skateboarding 26
standing up 11, 15
stilts 13
table balances 17, 19
tiptoe 11
toothbrush 14
toppling over 16, 17, 27
tower 16, 17, 27
toys to make 17, 18, 19
tray balances 20, 21
uneven blocks 12
water 12, 25

Guide to experiments

The notes below briefly outline the scientific principles underlying the experiments and include suggestions for alternative equipment to use and activities to try.

Can you balance? 10-11

Children find that activities such as standing on one leg can cause their bodies to topple over. This is because the mass of the body is subjected to the force of gravity. To balance, children must adjust the position of their bodies, so that their center of gravity (also known as center of mass) is directly above their balancing point.

Can you balance on things? 12-13

Children experiment further with their own center of gravity by balancing on various objects. Lowering their center of gravity, for instance by crouching down on the uneven blocks, increases the stability of their bodies. Another activity children can try is balancing on a football.

Will it balance? 14-15

These activities demonstrate that inanimate objects are also subject to the force of gravity. Children will need to adjust the position of an object and find its balancing point to stop it from toppling over. Other objects that children can balance on one finger or hand include a pencil, a spoon, and a tennis racket.

Will it topple over? 16-17

Widening the base of a tower gives it a lower center of gravity, which makes it more stable. In the toppling toy experiment, the modeling clay inside the lid makes the base heavier. This lowers the lid's center of gravity, making it very difficult to knock over. (Use a curved lid, such as that found on some anti-perspirant containers.)

Does it balance? 18-19

Hanging objects balance when their center of gravity is directly below their balancing points. Hence, in the dog-on-a-leash toy, the lightness of the cork is irrelevant, provided that the clay is positioned directly under the cork and toothpicks – the balancing point. A potato can be used instead of modeling clay in this experiment.

Will the tray balance? 20-21

Balancing a tray on one hand gives children further opportunities to look at balancing points.

When balancing a tray on a rolling pin, it helps if the rolling pin is secured to a flat surface with modeling clay. A heavy object can be made to balance a lighter object by moving the heavy object nearer to the pivot (the rolling pin) and the lighter object farther away from the pivot.

Can you make a mobile? 22-23

Mobiles depend upon heavy objects near the balancing point balancing lighter objects far from the balancing point. To make a mobile, the correct balancing point for each object has to be found. Children will need to readjust the position of the objects on their mobile every time they add a new object.

Will the buckets balance? 24-25

The bucket-balance demonstrates how mass and gravity are connected to balance. As well as the items shown, children could try putting stones, sand, or marbles in the buckets.

How well can you balance? 26-27

These experiments allow children to use the different balancing skills they have developed. The leg-lifting activity is impossible to do. Children will find that they cannot keep their center of gravity over their feet without moving their foot away from the wall.

29